by David Sabino
illustrated by Setor Fiadzigbey

Ready-to-Read

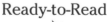

SIMON SPOTLIGHT
An imprint of Simon & Schuster Children's Publishing Division
New York   London   Toronto   Sydney   New Delhi
1230 Avenue of the Americas, New York, New York 10020
This Simon Spotlight edition August 2020
Copyright © 2019 by Simon & Schuster, Inc.
All rights reserved, including the right of reproduction in whole or in part in any form.
SIMON SPOTLIGHT, READY-TO-READ, and colophon are registered trademarks of Simon & Schuster, Inc.
For information about special discounts for bulk purchases, please contact Simon & Schuster Special Sales
at 1-866-506-1949 or business@simonandschuster.com.
Manufactured in China 0520 LEO

GLOSSARY

ASSIST: A pass that leads directly to a goal

BICYCLE KICK: A kick made with both feet in the air and usually above the head, where the ball ends up behind the kicker

BREAKAWAY: When a player moves past all the defenders, leaving just the goalkeeper between the player and the goal

BUNDESLIGA: The top professional men's soccer league in Germany

CLEAR: Moving the ball away from your team's goal

CORNER KICK: A free kick taken from the corner of the opponent's end of the field

DEAD BALL: When play is stopped and the ball stands still

DEFENDERS: Players whose primary role is to prevent the opposing team from scoring goals. There are four types of defenders: center-back, sweeper, full-back, and wing-back.

DRIBBLING: Controlling the ball while running

FIELD (OR PITCH): The area where the game is played. The field is made up of two halves with a goal on each goal line.

FOOTBALL: Another name for soccer, used in most places outside the United States

FORWARDS: The players nearest the opposing team's goal who are therefore most responsible for scoring goals

GOAL LINE: A line in front of a goalpost where a team attempts to advance the ball to score a goal

GOALKEEPER (OR GOALIE): The player who protects the goal from the other team's scoring tries

HANDBALL: A violation called when any player other than the goalkeeper touches the ball with their hand. This leads to a loss of possession, or even a penalty kick. A goalkeeper may be penalized for touching the ball with his/her hands outside of the goal area.

LA LIGA: The top professional soccer league in Spain

LINESMAN: An official who runs along the touchlines (also called sidelines) and watches for in- and out-of-bounds plays and fouls

MAJOR LEAGUE SOCCER (MLS): The top professional men's soccer league in the United States and Canada

MIDFIELDERS: Players who are generally positioned on the field between their team's defenders and forwards

OFFSIDE: A violation called when a player receives a pass with fewer than two defenders between the player and the goal

OWN GOAL: When the ball is accidentally scored against the player's own team

PENALTY KICK (OR PENALTY SHOT): A free kick at the goal from a spot twelve yards from the center of the other team's goal

PREMIER LEAGUE: The top professional men's soccer league in England

RED CARD: A penalty given for unsportsmanlike conduct in which that player is removed from the game

REFEREE: The lead official who enforces all the rules of the game and determines when periods will end. The referee is always positioned among the players on the field.

TACKLE: The use of feet or shoulders to try to take the ball away from the opponent

TOUCHLINES: The lines running along the edges of the field between the goal lines, also known as sidelines

UNITED STATES WOMEN'S NATIONAL TEAM (USWNT): The top women's soccer league in the United States

YELLOW CARD: A warning given to a player for unsportsmanlike conduct. A player who recieves two yellow cards is removed from the game.

Hello! My name is Michelle.
I'm the equipment manager for
a soccer team called the Dragons.
I'm in charge of the team's uniforms,
shoes, soccer balls, and all the other
things the players use
before and during a game.

I am heading to the field for today's
game against the Stars.
Before the game I will meet Ruby,
a new forward who was
just traded to our team.
Want to come along?

I love soccer, and many other people love soccer too.
In fact, soccer is the most popular sport in the world.
About four *billion* people are soccer fans.

That is a lot of people!
Soccer is so popular, astronauts
have even played it in space!

Soccer is played worldwide.
It is called "football"
in many countries.

In the United States
there is another game called football.
Soccer and American football are
very different from each other.

This is the stadium where
the Dragons play.
We go through a special gate
for the players, coaches, and
everyone who works here.

I head to the Dragons' locker room,
where I help players get ready.
Ruby has arrived!

I welcome Ruby to the team.
She is assigned her locker.
I give her a uniform and
the shoes soccer players
wear during the game.
The shoes have cleats (hard rubber
pieces) on the bottom to help
players run on the grass.

As the equipment manager, I make sure the players have everything they need before practice and each game. Shorts, jerseys with names and numbers on the back, long socks, and shin guards are just some of the gear I keep in a special closet.

I collect the equipment after every game and practice session. Then I wash the uniforms and clean the grass out of the cleats.

Sophia is warming up.
She is the goalkeeper for the Dragons.
She stops the other team from
scoring by keeping the ball out
of her team's goal.
The big painted box in front of the
goal is called the penalty area.
Only the goalkeeper can touch the
ball with her hands in that area.

The referee needs to tell the goalie apart from the players, so Sophia wears a different jersey than her team's. She also gets padded gloves. They protect her hands from very hard kicks.

Fans get to their seats with the help
of people called ushers.
Soccer fans have a lot of fun
at games.

Many of them wear the same colors as the team they are rooting for, and a lot of them have the same jerseys as the players.

Some fans bring banners, and sometimes the best banners are shown on the stadium scoreboard.

The players are getting ready for the game on the field.
I make sure there are enough soccer balls for everyone to warm up.
One of the balls is flat,
so I take out a pump and add air.

Groundskeepers paint the lines on the field. The lines on the short sides of the field are called goal lines. That is where the goal nets are placed.
The long sides of the field are called the touchlines, or sidelines.
The ball is out-of-bounds
when it goes outside those lines.

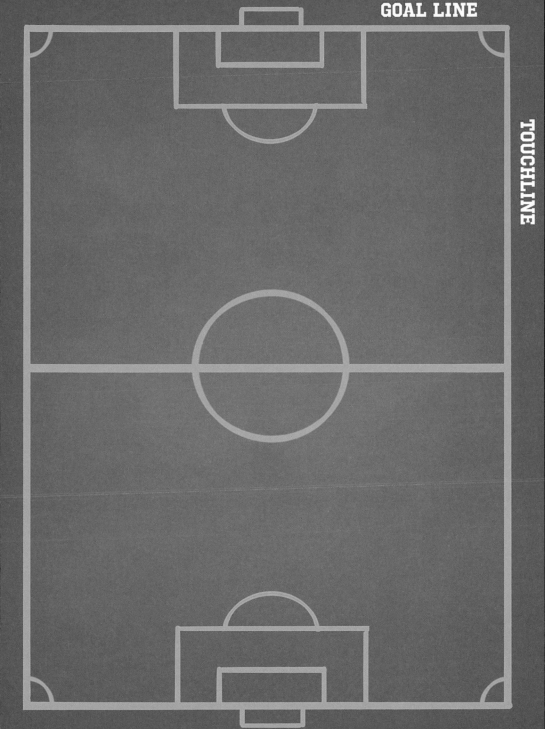

GOAL LINE

TOUCHLINE

When a ball goes out-of-bounds, a player stands just behind the touchline with both feet on the ground, holds the ball over her head with both hands, and throws it onto the field.

I can be found on the sidelines
during the game.
I sit there with the coaches and
extra players.
Trainers also sit with us.

Trainers help the players stretch
so they don't pull muscles.
Medics help if someone gets hurt,
and make sure that everyone has
water, especially on hot days.

I make sure that trainers have
any equipment or supplies
they might need.
I move around a lot during the game

Soccer fields are very large.
Our field is 120 yards long and
80 yards wide.
Each team typically has eleven
players on the field at one time.

GOAL LINE

GOALKEEPER

DEFENDER   DEFENDER   DEFENDER   DEFENDER

MIDFIELDER   MIDFIELDER   MIDFIELDER

FORWARD   FORWARD   FORWARD

TOUCHLINE

120 YARDS

FORWARD   FORWARD   FORWARD

MIDFIELDER   MIDFIELDER   MIDFIELDER

DEFENDER   DEFENDER   DEFENDER   DEFENDER

GOALKEEPER

80 YARDS

Each player does a special job
in their part of the field.
Defenders help the goalie keep the
other team from scoring.

Midfielders try to stop the other team from scoring and try to score for their team.

Forwards primarily try to score goals.

The referees make sure coaches and players follow the rules, and they also keep track of all the goals.

Most soccer games are ninety minutes long, but the referee can add time to the game to make up for any time the ball is not in play.

It's time for the game to begin.
The referee calls both teams
to the center of the field and makes
sure everyone is wearing
the equipment I gave them.
Then I hand the referee a special
game ball so we can begin the game.
The team that gets the ball is
determined by a coin toss between
captains of both teams.

Everybody is ready to play.
The referee places the ball
at the center of the field.
He blows the whistle and
the game clock starts.
The ball is in play!

The Stars pass the ball around and try to kick it past Sophia.
The ball bounces off Sophia's hands and flies high over the net.
The ball goes out-of-bounds.

Sophia starts the play
with a goal kick.
She lines the ball up on the edge
of the penalty area, then
she kicks it far down the field.

Ruby gets the ball and moves it past
two Stars defenders.
It's a breakaway!
Ruby dribbles ahead and
takes a shot.
It flies past the Stars' goalkeeper
into the net.
The Dragons score and
the crowd goes wild!

TEN COOL FACTS ABOUT SOCCER

1. The word "soccer" comes from England in the 1800s. The word "as**soc**iation" in the sport's official name (football association) gradually became shortened to "soccer."

2. To make them round, soccer balls are made by sewing together exactly thirty-two panels. Twenty of the panels are six-sided shapes (hexagons), and the other twelve are five-sided shapes (pentagons).

3. With four billion fans worldwide, soccer is the most popular sport in the world.

4. FIFA (Fédération Internationale de Football Association) is the organization that runs soccer worldwide. It's often called the United Nations of soccer, as its members represent 211 countries.

5. Games like soccer have been around for thousands of years, but the rules of soccer as we know them were first written down in 1863 in England.

6. Nations from all over the world compete for the FIFA World Cup. Men and women compete in separate tournaments every four years.

7. Based on Twitter followers, Cristiano Ronaldo from Portugal is the most popular athlete in the world. He has more than seventy-five million followers. That's almost thirty-four million more than basketball player LeBron James, in second place.

8. Soccer has been an Olympic sport since 1900. Men from the United States last won a medal in 1904. But the US Women's National Team has won four of the six gold medals given since Olympic women's soccer began in 1996.